Out My
Window

Out My *Window*

Ginger

XULON PRESS

Xulon Press
2301 Lucien Way #415
Maitland, FL 32751
407.339.4217
www.xulonpress.com

Paperback ISBN-13: 978-1-6628-1618-5
Ebook ISBN-13: 978-1-6628-1619-2

Table of Contents

FALL

WINTER

Introduction:
Out My Window

Looking out a window is a source of joy and encouragement to me, and I am often moved to write about whatever I am seeing. Sometimes, I am at home looking out a window. At other times, I am looking out my car window, the window of a vacation home, or out from a patio. At still other times, I have written just because whatever I am experiencing has led me to write.

This experience of writing has been a time of drawing closer to God, acknowledging Him as the master creator, provider, and protector of the beauty I have seen. It has led me to worship, praise, and thank Him for all His gifts.

The book has been a long time in the making, and it would not have happened without the encouragement of many friends over the years. I cannot name them for fear of omitting even one, but they know who they are. Please know that I am incredibly grateful. One friend I must mention. Jimmie Nell Spivey did some editing and, most importantly, shared some writing tips. She has my utmost appreciation. My daughter, Heidi Moore, has been the technology guru. I desperately needed help in that area, and she willingly gave of her time and expertise. Finally, I am grateful for my granddaughter, Claire, who did the four seasonal illustrations.

The devotionals which follow are based on the four seasons of the year. Each season is unique and brings new opportunities for praise and worship of the Master Creator.

I have written from my heart. I trust readers will read with theirs. My prayer is that they will be blessed as they read.

Ginger

Spring

Daffodils

First Day of Spring

It's spring! The calendar says so, and it makes me incredibly happy. A short ride today proved that spring has truly arrived. The trees are unbelievably beautiful. The leaves are budding out in that special spring green color. There are redbud trees, tulip trees, and pear, peach, and cherry trees. What a smorgasbord of color! White, pink, red, purple, and green. I am so grateful for this blessing and gift from the Creator.

> *Holy, holy, holy is the LORD Almighty; the whole earth is full of his glory. Isaiah 6:3b*

Thank You, God, that Your creation always glorifies You. Thank You that I can love You, praise You, and glorify You also. Accept my praise and gratitude for all of Your gifts.

Dogwood Tree

My dogwood tree is in bloom, and that brings me joy. I love examining the blossoms because they make me think of Easter. The four petals of each blossom form a cross. The edges of the blossoms have an indention which is tipped in red and resembles a blood-stained nail print. I love that the blossoms appear first and the green leaves, representing new life, appear afterward. What a picture of the crucifixion and the resurrection!

> *It was the third hour when they crucified him... So Joseph bought some linen cloth, took down the body, wrapped it in the linen, and placed it in a tomb cut out of rock. Mark 15:25,46*

> *You are looking for Jesus the Nazarene, who was crucified. He has risen! He is not here. See the place where they laid him. Mark 16:6*

LORD, I am thankful that Your creation reminds me of You and of Your sacrifice. Even as I am enjoying all the beauty, make me truly and humbly grateful.

Spring

Gratitude

"**Good morning,** Buddy." I greet the bluebird each morning when he comes to the feeder. He doesn't acknowledge my presence; nor does he appreciate the fact that I am the provider of the mealworms he loves to eat.

God, sometimes I feel that I treat you the same way the bluebird treats me. I visit with you for short periods of time and don't always acknowledge that you are the provider of all that I need.

> *You are my God, and I will give you thanks; you are my God, and I will exalt you. Give thanks to the LORD, for he is good; his love endures forever. Psalms 118:28-29*

Make me grateful, LORD, each day and each hour. You are so incredibly good to me.

Excitement

Wow! I just saw the first hummingbird of this spring. He is beautiful and quite a surprise. I don't have my feeder out yet, but that's all right, because God is feeding the little one without my help this morning. A gorgeous amaryllis is in full bloom just outside my window. It has outdone itself this season. Just one stem has six huge deep burgundy blooms on it, and the hummingbird has found it. What fun it is to watch him as his wings flutter at that astonishing rate. What a joy! What a gift! What a creator! It is amazing what He has done.

> *How many are your works, O LORD! In wisdom you made them all; the earth is full of your creatures. Psalms 104:24*

Thank You, God, that You give such amazing beauty and abundant joy to Your children.

Daffodils

As I drive along the roads today and see patches of yellow daffodils in bloom, I remember a day when I was in a field of daffodils. It was a huge field, and the flowers were without number. My friend and I were cutting blossoms to take back to our homes, but it didn't matter how many we cut. We didn't make a dent in the number of blooms. What a magnificent display of beauty! What a marvelous Creator who could engineer such a masterpiece. What a gift He gives us as we enjoy His creation each day.

> *Shout with joy to God, all the earth! Sing the glory of his name; make his praise glorious! Say to God "How awesome are your deeds!"*
> *Psalms 66:1-3a*

God, make me mindful of the gifts You give me each day, and create a grateful spirit within me. You are so good to me. You give me so many gifts. Thank you, God.

Washed Clean

God washed His world last night. Everything is sparkling, wet, and clean this morning. It was a good rainstorm, so all of the dust, pollen, and grime are washed off the trees, grass, and flowers.

The red tulips are absolutely glowing; the tulip tree is covered in deep pink blooms; and the white blossoms of the dogwood trees are just beginning to open. What a beautiful sight!

It is such a wonderful feeling to know that I can be washed clean, too. I get an opportunity today for a fresh start. God's grace allows me to begin this day knowing that all of my past sins are forgiven. I can feel clean and refreshed.

> *Cleanse me with hyssop, and I will be clean;*
> *wash me, and I will be whiter than snow.*
> *Psalms 51:7*

LORD, help me to walk this day thankful for the blessing of Your grace and forgiveness.

Storms

༈

The sky is depressing this morning. Dark clouds are hiding any sign of a sun, and the rain is torrential. For several days it has been raining, and the forecast is for even more. The winds are strong enough to make me feel uneasy, and the view out my window matches the feelings in my heart.

I am reminding myself that the sun is shining some-where, and the rain will stop soon. I can find hope and joy in the midst of this storm.

> *He made the earth by his power; he founded the world by his wisdom and stretched out the heavens by his understanding. When he thun-ders, the waters in the heavens roar; he makes clouds rise from the ends of the earth. He sends lightning with the rain and brings out the wind from his storehouses. Jeremiah 51:15-16*

God, help me to remember that You created the storms, and that You are in control. Help me to trust in Your goodness, this day and always.

Blessed

The Carolina wren is a little brown bird. Nothing about it attracts a lot of attention, but one of them makes me smile every day. This little wren has made a nest in a flowerpot that a squirrel tipped over last winter. About eight feet away from the nest is a bluebird feeder. Who knew that the wren would love mealworms so much? I tell her that I have the food there for the bluebirds, but she pays no attention to me. Between the nest and the feeder is a hanging basket full of colorful pansies. The wren visits the flowers daily. I believe she thinks she has her own private resort.

Oftentimes, I feel that God has blessed me with my own private resort. My home fills me with comfort, and I am surrounded by friends and family. Flowers bloom in my yard, and birds visit every day. What joy! What a blessing!

> *Taste and see that the LORD is good; blessed is the man who takes refuge in him. Psalms 34:8.*

LORD, I am overwhelmingly grateful this day. Help me to always trust in You as my source of blessings.

A Rose

A friend brought me a beautiful red rose today. It was the first rose on their bush this season, so I felt truly honored. This was a cold and windy day, and I was feeling a little blue. What a special blessing that thoughtful gift was! It is a treat to see that beauty sitting on my desk as I work!

Friends are surely a gift from God. Sometimes I feel like they are angels in disguise. I read once that friends are God's vehicle for His grace. What a great idea from a great God.

> *A friend loves at all times. Proverbs 17:17*

> *Two are better than one, because they have a good return for their work: If one falls down, his friend can help him up. Ecclesiates 4:9*

LORD, help me to truly appreciate each friend as a gift from You. Help me to be the friend to others that You would have me be today.

Iris

They come in many colors, but these are the purest white. Their brilliance is stunning, and I am in awe. There can be no purer white in nature than these irises. I recall the expression, "White as the driven snow," but these irises appear whiter than snow. The wool of sheep is known to be white, but I've never seen wool as white as these flowers.

White has always symbolized purity and I am reminded today of the absolute purity of my Savior. God's only son, pure and undefiled, was sacrificed for me.

> *"Come now, let us reason together," says the LORD. Though your sins are like scarlet, they shall be as white as snow; though they are red as crimson, they shall be as wool. Isaiah 1:18*

Thank You, LORD, for this reminder of Your purity and Your gift of unconditional forgiveness.

Easter

What joy! What excitement! I am gathered with other Christians on a hillside watching the sun as it rises to greet the day. There is a perfect reflection in the lake which lies below us. The songs ring out over the land, "I Serve a Risen Savior," "He Lives, He Lives," and "Up from the Grave He Arose." The cries of "He's Alive, He's Alive," echo across the lake. My heart is thrilled to be a part of this Easter sunrise service. I am celebrating the greatest event in the history of the world, and I can hardly contain the emotion that fills me. This day is a gift, a day of joy, a day of remembrance, and a day of gratitude.

> *...the men said to them, "Why do you look for the living among the dead? He is not here; he has risen! Luke 24:5b-6*

HALLELUJAH! AMEN!

A Bad Hair Day

The little cardinal makes me laugh. He is bright red, as all male cardinals are, but the crest on his head looks thin, scraggly, and unkempt. You talk about a bad hair day! I know it will grow and settle into a beautiful addition to his appearance, but I will laugh each time I see him until he matures.

Bad hair days happen, but I'm thinking about things other than hair. I'm thinking about days when nothing seems to go right, when everything I do just doesn't turn out the way I expect, or the way I want it to. Then I can only take a deep breath, realize I'm not in control, and count my many blessings.

> *Praise be to the Lord, to God our Savior, who daily bears our burdens.* Psalms 68:19

Lord, help me to rely on You for peace in the midst of trying times. You are in control. Help me to trust in Your love and tender care each and every day.

Spring

Sparkling Morning

I am amazed by the sparkling display I am seeing this morning. Each blade of grass seems to have its own little colorful bubble of water just sitting there waiting to be absorbed. It is a delightful sight.

I know that the day which lies ahead will be another scorcher, but this morning is cool, and I am enjoying the gift. I am smiling as I remember that the Creator once watered his earth with just the morning dew. No need for rain in the garden, just the gentle watering by the dew. What a master gardener!

> *When the LORD God made the earth and the*
> *heavens—the LORD God had not yet sent rain*
> *on the earth—streams came up from the earth*
> *and watered the whole surface of the ground.*
> Genesis 2:4-6

Thank You, God, for the refreshing start to this new day. Thank You for Your creative blessings.

Summer

Cardinal

First Day of Summer

I am happy to greet this day at an early hour. It is the first day of summer and is the longest day of the year. The sun is up, and the morning is lovely, but I know that for the next six months, each day will be shorter than the last. I do so enjoy the long days. When the shorter days come, the pleasant evenings are missed. It is wonderful that we can know the seasons and can anticipate the uniqueness of each one. We have studied the cycles of the sun and moon, and we are certain that the seasons will come and go as they were planned.

> *Give thanks to the Lord, for He is good… who made the great lights-the sun to govern the day, the moon and stars to govern the night.*
> Psalms 136:1,7-9

Thank You, God, that You set the sun, moon, and stars in place. Thank You that You govern the seasons. Help me to enjoy each season as You have planned it.

Titmouse

I love the little titmouse. This bird is attractively designed in black and gray, with a bit of rust on its sides. Beady black eyes, a tufted crest, and a bright expression are attention getting, but what attracts me most are its eating habits. It comes to the feeder, takes one seed, and flies away. In a short while, it returns for one more seed. I wonder how it gets enough nourishment from the one seed to merit the flights, but that is its routine. What a contrast to the other birds which often sit and gorge themselves!

> *Be on your guard against all kinds of greed; a man's life does not consist in the abundance of his possessions.* Luke 12:15

Lord, this day, help me to appreciate Your gifts. Create in me a profoundly grateful heart with a spirit of contentment.

Summer

Angels

Four cardinals are in the yard today. The birds are always bright and beautiful and a source of joy to me.

A very common saying is, "Cardinals appear when angels are near." If that is so, I am truly blessed. It is nice to consider that angels may be around when those red birds appear, but I don't need cardinals to experience the blessings of the angels who are present in my life.

> *Do not forget to entertain strangers, for by so doing some people have entertained angels without knowing it. Hebrews 13:2*

Thank You, LORD, that Your angels are often in my presence to minister to me, to comfort me, and to draw me close to You.

Evening Songs

$\mathcal{S}uch\ a$ pleasant evening! Daylight is fading; clouds are forming, promising rain; and the birds are chirping and singing. I wonder what they are singing about. Are they calling for their mates to come home for the night? Are they chatting about the great day they just enjoyed? Are they talking about the great food source they have found, or are they simply singing praises to their Creator?

Praising God is a great way to end a day. It leads to a wonderful night of refreshing rest. Those praises crowd out worries and let peace reign in my mind and heart. I will go to sleep grateful for God's wonderful love, mercy, and grace.

> Praise the LORD. How good it is to sing praises to our God, how pleasant and fitting to praise him! Psalms 147:1

Thank You, LORD, that I can lift praises to You at any time. What a privilege to enjoy a time of fellowship with You. Thank You for Your gifts of rest and the peace that passes all understanding.

Zinnias

I love the summer months. It's true that some-times it is much too hot for my comfort. It's also true that planting and tending a flower garden is really tiring and hard work, but the satisfaction is wonderful. Today my zinnias are in full bloom. There are so many of them, and such a variety of colors, but the most beautiful sight of all is an orange and black butterfly which is flitting among the blossoms. I feel like it is a special gift from God for this day.

> *I know that there is nothing better for men to be happy and do good while they live. That everyone may eat and drink and find satisfaction in all his toil—this is the gift of God. Ecclesiastes 3: 12-13*

Lord, remind me to recognize and appreciate that every good gift is from You.

Stars

Oh, the stars! I am in awe. I am speechless. There are so many. I am at the bottom of the Grand Canyon where there is no light from human sources. The entire scope of heaven is covered with stars. I have never seen so many. There must be millions, and I have never seen them. Look! There is a shooting star, and another, and another! What a glorious display of heavenly bodies. This sight will be seared on my memory for as long as I live.

> *God made two great lights—the greater light to govern the day and the lesser light to govern the night. He also made the stars. God set them in the expanse of the sky to give light on the earth… and God saw that it was good. Genesis 1:16-18*

Thank You, God, for showing me Your astounding creation this night. I praise Your name and give You praise for being the creator.

Ocean

I am in awe every time I see it. It is so powerful, so enormous. My eyes can't take it all in. And the sound! The unceasing roar of the waves crashing on the beach. Yes, unceasing. The waves just keep coming nonstop. I see them forming far away from the shore, and I sense the power in that wall of water. I know the ocean doesn't go on forever, but as I stand on the sand and feel the spray of saltwater on my face, it seems unending. What an omnipotent creator.

> *"And God said, 'Let the water under the sky be gathered in one place, and let dry ground appear. And it was so. God called the dry ground land, and the gathered waters he called seas." Genesis 1:9-10*

Lord, help me this day to remember again that You are indeed the creator of this world and everything in it that is good. I praise Your all-knowing and all-powerful presence.

Summer

Nuthatch

What a crazy sight! That little bird is walking down the tree trunk headfirst! How does he do that? He is a striking bird with a black cap and beady black eyes on a white face, but nothing demands attention as much as his ability to walk headfirst down the tree trunk. He must have very strong feet. He is unique. I wonder why God made him that way. I wonder what his special purpose is.

I am convinced that each of God's creations has a unique purpose. I read once that man is the only one of God's creations that lives in rebellion to His will. Isn't that amazing? Why would I do that? Do I not believe that I would be happiest if I lived according to the purpose for which I was made?

> *For I know the plans I have for you, declares the LORD, plans to prosper you and not to harm you, plans to give you a hope and a future. Jeremiah 29:11*

LORD, help me to seek and follow Your will today.

Summer

Hummingbird

My heart is happy this morning. A female hummingbird is at the feeder, and though a window separates us, she seems really close. I wonder if she has babies somewhere near.

Occasionally, she stops feeding and looks straight at me as if to say, "Thank you." It makes me smile, and I whisper, "You're welcome." What a blessing this beautiful hummingbird is to me this morning.

> *O LORD my God, I will give you thanks forever.*
> *Ps. 30:12b*

I am considering how often I stop and thank God for the blessings that He provides. My heart knows that He is the giver of all good gifts. May my prayer be full of thanksgiving.

Bluebirds

The baby bluebirds left their nest. I have checked on them from the time the parents started building the nest. The eggs were laid. The mother kept them warm, and the babies hatched out. Then I loved watching the male and the female as they flitted around the yard gathering food for the little ones. This morning, I was really feeling poorly. As I sat in my recliner, the beautiful male bluebird perched on my window and took a good look inside. As this is not typical behavior, I felt like he was checking on me. It made me smile.

What a comfort the little bird was! What joy he brought to me! Was he an angel in disguise? Was he a messenger?

> *Are not all angels ministering spirits sent to serve those who will inherit salvation? Hebrews 1:14*

God, I thank You for the beautiful bird You created and sent to me this morning. Use me today to bring joy and comfort to others as You have comforted me.

Summer

Waterfall

I left the heat of the valley today and drove into the mountains. The woods are bursting with life. The deer are grazing, and the birds are darting among the trees. I saw a little rabbit munching in the grass, and I know there are bears around, even though I don't know where they might be.

But there is a sight to behold! The water is thundering over a cliff and is beautiful. The noise is almost deafening, and there is a rainbow in the mist. The spray is cool and moist. I absolutely love it and am awed by the power that is displayed. The Creator blessed me with this spectacular sight.

> *As the rain and snow come down from heaven,*
> *and do not return to it without watering*
> *the earth and making it bud and flourish,...*
> *Isaiah 55:10*

God, today I stand in awe of Your wisdom, Your creativity, Your steadfastness, and Your love.

Faith

The hummingbirds are busy entertaining
me this morning. They are putting on a show. They
zoom; they hover; they soar; they fly up and then
down. Amazing is the only word that describes them.
They love my feeder, but they don't trust me. If I am
in sight, they approach the feeder and then fly away.
The food is there for them, but they are tenuous.
Thankfully, some birds are feeding even though
they see me. I bless the birds with an ample supply
of food. It is there for the taking. Their lack of faith
in me denies them the benefit which is offered.

> *Praise the LORD, O my soul, and forget not
> all his benefits—who forgives all your sins and
> heals all your diseases, ...who crowns you with
> love and compassion, who satisfies your desires
> with good things. Psalms 103:2-5*

Increase my faith LORD so that I will enjoy the ben-
efits You offer.

Summer

Colors that Amaze

Yellow is the dominant color in my yard this morning: the golden sun, the goldfinches, the sunflowers, the giant zinnias, and the butterflies. What a feast for the eyes! Other colors are here, too: pinks, purples, and reds.

The Creator had a giant palette of colors when He created our world. Every shade, hue, and tint came from His hand. He blessed us with the myriad colors we see everyday.

> *For you make me glad for your deeds, O LORD; I sing for joy at the works of your hands. Psalms 92:4*

My heart is singing today. Thank You for the blessing of color.

Fall

Pumpkin

Autumn

First Day of Fall

It's official. Fall is here at last, and I am looking forward to cooler days, trips to apple country, and colors in the trees that will amaze. Pumpkins will appear and fall crops will be harvested. This special season has arrived as scheduled, and all that is anticipated about this season will come to pass.

On this day, every place on earth will have twelve hours of daylight and twelve hours of darkness. That only happens twice a year, and to think that God planned that at creation.

> *I will send you rain in its season, and the ground will yield its crops and the trees of the field their fruit. Leviticus 26:4*

Thank You, God, that in Your wisdom, You created the seasons. I praise You for the gifts of each one and celebrate the bounty which You provide.

Autumn

All Things

God scrubbed His world clean last night. The rain was heavy and refreshing. Everything is sparkling this morning. The bright red of a cardinal is visible through the green pine branches. A bunny just hopped across the yard, and the titmouse is busy flitting back and forth between the feeder and the trees. I am reminded of the poem:

> *All Things Bright and Beautiful*
> *All creatures Great and Small*
> *All Things Wise and Wonderful*
> *The Lord God made them All.*

> *He has made everything beautiful in its time.*
> *Ecclesiastes 3:11*

Thank You, God, for Your gift of this day. Thank You that I have a quiet place where I can focus on You and Your blessings. Please, this day, create in me a heart which is always grateful.

Autumn

A Bountiful Feast

The Cardinal climber is finally blooming. The beautiful feathery green vine has been growing all summer, but I began to think that it would never bloom. Finally, hundreds of little red flowers are covering the vine, and the hummingbirds are loving it. They are genuinely enjoying a feast which has been spread before them.

> *The cheerful heart has a continual feast.*
> *Proverbs 15:15b*

Lord, this day help me to focus on the multitude of blessings You are providing. My heart will then be cheerful, and I will be feasting in Your presence.

Autumn

Balance

I am watching a squirrel this morning as he runs along a power line. He is really good at keeping his balance as he scurries along, and I am considering how he manages that. I notice that his tail keeps flipping back and forth as he runs, and I've decided that the tail is his secret. Isn't that amazing? This creature has a built in rudder that keeps him perfectly balanced on a very small wire.

I know that my creator gave me a rudder to help me keep my balance, too. I just don't use it as successfully as the squirrel does. Frequently I get things out of balance in my life. It's easy to let my priorities get out of order. It's a lot harder to keep them properly lined up. What sorts of things take first place in my life? A job? Family? Friends? Sports? Addictions? Bad habits?

> *The most important one (commandment) is this:*
> *...Love the LORD your God with all your heart*
> *and with all your soul and with all your strength.*
> *The second is this: Love your neighbor as your-*
> *self. Mark 12:29-31*

God remind me each day what my priorities should be and teach me how to maintain the proper balance in my life.

 *Autumn*

Joy

❧

It is a typical morning. I made coffee and am enjoying my first cup. I'm surprised by a sudden movement outside my window. It's a cardinal! I haven't seen one in quite a while, and my spirit is lifted as I quietly sit and watch. It is perfect! That bright red body is lighting up a dreary gray morning. I have read that a cardinal is a symbol of joy, and it is so true for me today. I am so thankful for that unexpected gift, a visit by one of God's beauties.

Rejoicing comes in the morning. Psalms 30:35

LORD, teach me to rejoice each day as I recognize Your gifts and blessings. Your love never fails, and Your mercy is unending. Thank You.

Rainfall

I am enjoying sitting on the patio this evening. It is almost dark, and the rain is a constant downpour. I am reminded of my childhood when I enjoyed making a warm and cozy place on the porch while it rained. I would drape a blanket over an overturned rocking chair and crawl inside where I felt snug, warm, secure, and comforted. I feel that way on the patio this evening, but I know the source of my security and comfort is not a makeshift cave made of a blanket. I feel secure in my relationship with my Creator and Savior.

> *Cast your cares on the LORD and he will sustain you; he will never let the righteous fall.*
> *Psalms 55:22*

Thank You, God, for all of the blessings You give. I am especially grateful this day for the comfort and peace You give during dark and stormy times. Help me to always trust in You. Teach me to cast all of my cares on You, for I know You do love and care for me

Thanksgiving

It is that time of year again, when one special day is set aside for giving thanks. I think about the origin of this day and remember the multiple times I studied the pilgrims and Indians. We recalled that story each year in school and as youngsters had fun with plays and celebrations.

I am grateful for the many times family and friends have gathered to celebrate this day. It has always been a time for feasting, fellowship, and football.

Today I will remember the old hymn which urged us to count our blessings, to name them one by one. I will remember to thank the giver of all blessings.

> *Give thanks to the LORD, call on his name;*
> *make known among the nations what he has*
> *done. Sing to him, sing praise to him; tell of all*
> *his wonderful acts. I Chronicles 16:8-9*

LORD, make me profoundly grateful this day. Help me to meditate on the truth that every good and perfect gift is from You.

Autumn

Sunrise

Wow, I almost missed it. The eastern sky was ablaze with color. The sun wasn't up yet, but its coming was announced in vivid oranges and pinks. The clouds which were interspersed completed the mural. It was so pretty, but it was fleeting. The sky faded to gray with only a touch of pink. Oh, it was beautiful. I'm thinking that when Christ returns, the sky will announce His coming in spectacular fashion. What a glorious day that will be!

> *I saw heaven standing open and there before me was a white horse, whose rider is called Faithful and True. His eyes are like blazing fire, and on his head are many crowns. On his robe and on his thigh he has this name written:*
>
> *KING OF KINGS AND LORD OF LORDS.*
>
> *Revelation 19:11-12,16*

Lord, remind me daily that You promised that You would return. Help me to live today as though I expect Your return at any moment.

Autumn

Mountains

I love the mountains in every season. In winter, they are covered in snow and filled with silence. In the spring, the trees are bursting with color and filled with the songs of birds. In the summer, the mountains bring cool relief from the heat of the valleys; and in the fall, they are bursting with foliage that takes your breath away. I go to the mountains to have my spirits uplifted and revived. When I can't go to the mountains, I think of them and experience joy in the memory.

> *I lift up my eyes to the hills—where does my help come from? My help comes from the LORD, the Maker of heaven and earth. Psalms 121:1-2*

Thank You, God.

Autumn

Squirrels

The squirrels are busy today. They are gathering the hickory nuts and acorns which are lying all over the ground. Obviously, they are preparing for winter. They know that cold weather is on its way. It isn't cold today. In fact, the weather is lovely. The trees haven't lost their leaves yet and are quite colorful, but the squirrels are storing up food for the hard days ahead. Isn't it amazing that the animals know so much about what they need to do to survive?

> *Go to the ant, you sluggard; consider its ways and be wise. It has no commander, no overseer or ruler, yet it stores its provisions in summer and gathers its food at the harvest.*
> *Proverbs 111:5*

God, give me wisdom so that I can know how You would have me work to provide for my needs as I rely on You for Your provision.

Autumn

Sunset

The sunset is beautiful beyond description; the heavens are exploding with color. It is breathtaking and overwhelming. In the midst of my admiration, I hear a dad saying, "Kids, have you said, 'Thank you, Jesus', for that awesome sunset?" The answer in my heart is, "No." I haven't been grateful. I've just been awed. I could have been praising God for this gift of beauty, but the thought had not crossed my mind.

> *I will give thanks to the LORD because of his righteousness and will sing praise to the name of the LORD most high. Psalms 17:7*

> *Give thanks to the LORD, for he is good; His love endures forever. Psalms 107:1*

> *God, I am so prone to take Your gifts for granted. Help me each day to ponder Your creativity, to appreciate Your provision, and to praise Your name.*

Autumn

Barn Swallows

I am watching the barn swallows as they swoop through the air. They eat multitudes of insects as they fly. Such beauties they are, blue-black above and cinnamon-buff colored below. I'm thankful for the gift of their beauty and that they do so well what they were created to do. I will miss the swallows when they leave for the winter and will look forward to their return in the spring. What a blessing they are to us humans!

> *Every good and perfect gift is from above, coming down from the Father of the heavenly lights who does not change like shifting shadows. James 1:17*

Thank You, God for each and every gift You give me. I am blessed beyond measure by Your provision, Your grace, Your mercy, and Your faithfulness

Autumn

Missing birds

So many birds are missing this morning. My beautiful yellow goldfinches, my Carolina chickadees, my little wrens, and others are not in my garden. I do see a pair of cardinals, and the amazing hummingbird is all over the blooms of the cardinal climber. I see the titmouse making his usual trips to the feeders, but I am sad that others are not here. Should I just complain about the missing birds, or should I be grateful and count the blessings that I am able to enjoy?

> *Let us be thankful and so worship God acceptably with reverence and awe. Hebrews 12:28b*

LORD, make me aware this day of the many blessings that You have showered on me. Thank You for your constant love and mercy. Thank You that You faithfully forgive and give me peace.

Winter

The Star

Winter Darkness

Today marks the official first day of winter, and it is the shortest day of the year. I will have so few hours of daylight today, and the rain is coming down in buckets. That adds to the darkness. How I am wishing for some sunshine!

I am excited, though, because, although it is dark and dreary today, I know that I will now begin to gain a few minutes of daylight each day. It will be a slow process, but before too long, I will be excited to see that nightfall comes later and dawn comes earlier. What a joy that will be!

> *You are my lamp, O LORD; the LORD turns my darkness into light. 2 Samuel 22:29*

LORD, I know that the seasons change at Your will. Help me to realize that You can be my light even when it is dark. Help me to know that You can change my darkness into light, whether my darkness is of my spirit, my mind, my soul, or my circumstances.

Hope

The sky is black this morning. Layers of dark clouds are covering every part of the heavens. I am watching and waiting for signs of sunrise. A pale pink streak is beginning to form between two cloud layers. It is exciting to watch as the sky gets a little brighter each moment. It is winter, and the trees are bare. I can only see the dark twisted shapes of the limbs against the emerging light

Wait! What are those moving shadows? Oh, squirrels are scurrying about spoiling my view. They remind me of doubts which sometimes sneak into my mind and heart, spoiling hopes I am embracing.

The LORD delights in those who fear him, who put their hope in his unfailing love. Psalms 147:11

Dear God, may my heart be so filled with hope that I cannot allow any doubts to steal the joy that comes from resting in Your love and promises.

Joy to the World

It is the Christmas season, that time of year when each day is filled with activity. What an opportunity to celebrate the greatest gift in the history of the world, the babe in the manger!

I join the congregation as we sing, "Oh, Come Let Us Adore Him." Accompanied by six baby grand pianos and twelve gifted musicians, the voices raised in praise and adoration make me feel as though I am tasting a little bit of heaven.

> *Then I heard every creature in heaven and on earth and under the earth and on the sea, and all that is in them, singing "To him who sits on the throne and to the Lamb be praise and honor and glory and power for ever and ever." Revelation 5:13*

God, in this busy season, help me to praise and celebrate You. Help me to have special times of worship, to be joyful, and to be grateful.

The Star

It is a crystal-clear night, and the stars are shining. I am thinking of the star that led the Magi to worship the Christ child. I love knowing that it was an actual astrological event where planets aligned themselves in such a way that they appeared to be one star. It thrills me to think that all of this was programmed in the heavens when creation occurred. What a Creator!

It is my favorite time of the year. I am anticipating the coming of Christmas. This season is called Advent, and it is not only a time for me to remember the birth of the Christ child, but it is also a time of preparing for the second coming of Christ.

> *Where is the one who has been born king of the Jews? We saw his star in the east and have come to worship him. Matthew 2:2*

> *I am going there to prepare a place for you...and I will come back to take you with me that you also may be where I am. John 14:2, 3*

Help me, LORD, to prepare my heart to celebrate the birth of Your son. Help me to cherish the presence of Christ in my life today and to look forward passionately to His coming again.

Christmas

It's that most wonderful time of the year. There is snow on the ground and a nip in the air. I have watched my favorite Christmas programs on TV, and a beautiful tree in my home is decorated with special ornaments. Gifts are wrapped and waiting under the tree; cheerful greetings are heard; and wishes for peace, joy, and love are shared.

I ponder the reason for the celebration amid the hustle and bustle, the decorating, and the gift giving, I remember that mankind is celebrating the one and only gift that all of mankind needs. I rejoice that the evergreen tree represents eternal life and that the traditional colors of Christmas, red, green and white, symbolize not only eternal life, but also the purity of Christ and the blood that was shed for our sins.

Today in the town of David a Savior has been born to you; He is Christ the LORD. Luke 2:11

LORD, as I celebrate, let me not forget the gift You gave, the gift of a Savior who is the giver of eternal life.

 *Winter*

Resurrection

Today, as I look out my window, I am seeing no evidence of life. There are no birds; the grass looks dead; and tree limbs are bare. It is depressing, but I know that soon the grass will start turning green; sap will start rising in the trees; and leaves will burst forth. I will be glad when that happens. Spring always brings a renewal of hope and a picture of the resurrection of life.

There exists a promise for an eternal life where there will be no more hunger, thirst, scorching heat, or tears.

Jesus told us:

> *"I am the resurrection and the life. He who believes in me will live, even though he dies."*
> *John 11:25*

LORD, lead me to live each day with the certain knowledge that I will one day be in your presence and that unparalleled joy will abound.

Protection

What a beautiful morning! My world is a pristine white, as everything is covered with snow. All the ugliness of winter, the dead grass, the barren soil, and the leafless trees, are covered. There is a bright red spot in this whiteness. A cardinal is resting in the shelter of the green leaves of the magnolia tree. What a sight!

I often think of the birds in winter and wonder where they find shelter. This cardinal was well sheltered in the branches. It looked calm, peaceful, and secure in nature's provision.

> *You have been a refuge for the poor, a refuge for the needy in his distress, a shelter from the storm, and a shade from the heat. Isaiah 25:4*

LORD, help me to learn to depend on Your love and provision even when storms come my way.

Provision

It is so cold this morning. Frost is everywhere. The little birds are scurrying around on the ground, flitting in the trees, and enjoying all the seeds, peanuts, and suet in the feeders. I'm seeing titmice, chickadees, a little woodpecker, goldfinches, and even a couple of juncos, and I'm so happy that I have plenty of food for them, but what about shelter? I have several bird houses in the yard, but the birds never seem to use them in the winter. How are they staying warm? Well, they do look a little fluffier than usual. Oh, yes. They don't need me to protect them. They are using the method God gave them to insulate themselves from the cold. What a creator! God provides and protects the little birds.

> *Are not two sparrows sold for a copper coin? And not one of them falls to the ground apart from your Father's will. But the very hairs of your head are numbered. Do not fear; therefore, you are of more value than many sparrows. Matthew 10:29-31*

My loving heavenly Father, help me this day to trust You for my provision and protection. Thank You for the assurance that I matter to You, that You value me, and that I can completely rely on You.

Space Station

It is a clear cold night, and I am standing in my yard watching the space station pass overhead. It appears so close that I can see what I think are the solar panels on the sides. I often consider that man could only have achieved success in the exploration of space by discovering and understanding the scientific principles that were established when our universe was created.

I am grateful that the astronaut, Buzz Aldrin, celebrated communion on the surface of the moon. The first liquid poured on the moon and the first food eaten on the moon's surface celebrated the sacrifice of God's son for the redemption of mankind.

> *Through him all things were made; without him nothing was made that has been made. John 1:3*

God, You made the stars, the sun, the moon, and gravity, and You sacrificed Your son for me. Thank you.

Winter

New Year's Day

It is a time for beginning anew. It is a special day with an opportunity to assess my relationships, my goals, and my priorities.

I will make no resolutions today regarding physical or productive goals. I will take this day which You have given me and live it to glorify You by my actions and my words.

> *This is the day the LORD has made; let us rejoice and be glad in it. Psalms 118:24*

God, help me this day to put You and Your will first in my life. Let Your spirit fill me and produce fruit which will bring glory to You in this new year.

A Snow Covered World

What a happy surprise! Snow fell overnight and left my world clean and white. Everything is calm, peaceful, and quiet. It is as though all sound has been muffled. I am genuinely happy and content.

It is a time to spend worshiping my creator with no noisy distractions. What a great gift this day is.

Before leaving this earth, Jesus promised:

> *Peace I leave with you; my peace I give you. I do not give to you as the world gives. Do not let your hearts be troubled and do not be afraid. John 14:27*

Thank You, LORD, for this day of beauty. Thank You for Your peace that You have given to those who love You. Thank You for the peace that passes all understanding.

 *Winter*

Master Creator

"*The sun,* with all these planets revolving around it and depending on it, can still ripen a bunch of grapes as if it had nothing else in the universe to do." Galileo

Galileo, the noted astronomer, physicist, engineer, and father of modern science who lived almost 400 years ago, recognized the amazing power of our star which we call the sun.

As I sit and watch the birds on this cold winter day, I am enjoying delicious red grapes which were shipped in from a warm climate. The sun ripened these grapes for me.

> *God made two lights-the greater light to govern the day and the lesser light to govern the night. Genesis 1:16*

God, You gave us everything we need when You created the universe. Make me aware and grateful for those gifts each day.

Crocuses

They are such tiny flowers. It is still winter, but these special blossoms have burst through the cold, lifeless ground. What a gift!

Three colors have appeared so far. The first ones were white; the next ones were yellow; and the last ones to appear were purple.

The colors symbolize much to me. The white ones represent the pure and sinless Savior. Yellow represents the marvelous creative power of Christ. Purple reminds me that I am a child of the King. What joy these little flowers bring!

> *For everything God created is good. I Timothy 4:4*

How thankful I am today that You are indeed my Savior, my creator, and the giver of all perfect gifts.

About the author

❧

Virginia (Ginger) Yearwood Long was born and raised in Atlanta, Georgia. She received a Bachelor of Arts degree in Science with concentrations in chemistry and biology from Tift College in Forsyth, Georgia. Most of her working life has been as a teacher in the states of Florida, Alaska, and Georgia. In between her teaching positions, she has served as a bookkeeper, tax preparer, medical research technician, serology lab technician, and various other positions. As her first book is being published, she remembers that she has often said that she still does not know what she wants to do when she grows up.

Ginger presently resides in Canton, GA where she is near her two daughters and six grandchildren.

CPSIA information can be obtained
at www.ICGtesting.com
Printed in the USA
LVHW111925100921
697556LV00005B/368

9 781662 816185